SAVE THE ANIMALS

ORANGUTAN ORPHANS

Clare Hibbert

PowerKiDS
press.

New York

Published in 2015 by
The Rosen Publishing Group, Inc.
29 East 21st Street, New York, NY 10010

Library of Congress Cataloging-in-Publication Data

Hibbert, Clare, 1970- author.
 Orangutan orphans / Clare Hibbert.
     pages cm. — (Save the animals)
 Includes bibliographical references and index.
 ISBN 978-1-4777-5905-9 (pbk.)
 ISBN 978-1-4777-5901-1 (6 pack)
 ISBN 978-1-4777-5906-6 (library binding)
1. Sepilok Orang Utan Rehabilitation Centre—
Juvenile literature. 2. Nyaru Menteng Orangutan
Rescue and Rehabilitation Center (Borneo)—
Juvenile literature. 3. Orangutans—Infancy—
Borneo—Juvenile literature. 4. Orangutans—
Reintroduction—Borneo—Juvenile literature. 5.
Orangutans—Habitat—Conservation—Juvenile
literature. 6. Wildlife conservation—Borneo—
Juvenile literature. 7. Wildlife reintroduction—
Juvenile literature. I. Title.
 QL737.P94H53 2015
 599.88'3—dc23
                              2014026399

Copyright © 2015 by
The Rosen Publishing Group, Inc.

First published in 2015 by Franklin Watts
Copyright © Arcturus Holdings Limited

Editor: Joe Harris
Picture researcher: Clare Hibbert
Designer: Tokiko Morishima

Picture credits: all images Eric Baccega/Nature PL
except pages 2–3: Pete Oxford/Nature PL and pages
5 (bg) and 14-15 (bg): Shutterstock. Cover image:
Pete Oxford/Nature PL

Manufactured in the United States of America
CPSIA Compliance Information: Batch #CW15PK: For Further Information contact
Rosen Publishing, New York, New York at 1-800-237-9932

CONTENTS

SAVING ORANGUTANS

The rainforest-covered islands of Borneo and Sumatra are home to a very special great ape, the orangutan. Sadly, the number of orangutans is falling. Different organizations work in the forests to help save these amazing animals.

The oldest center dedicated to helping orangutans is the Sepilok Orangutan Sanctuary on the edge of what is now the Kabili Forest Reserve. It was founded around 50 years ago and is in the Malaysian part of Borneo. The Sepilok staff nurses sick or orphaned orangutans back to health and then rehabilitate them. That means getting them ready to return to normal life. Most orangutans are released back into a national park or reserve.

10-year-old Thomas is cared for at Camp Leakey.

The Indonesian part of Borneo has its own centers. Camp Leakey, in the Tanjung Puting National Park, has been running for more than 40 years. It was named after Louis Leakey, a famous anthropologist – an expert in the study of human societies. He made exciting discoveries about early humans that showed their connection with great apes. Other centers include the Nyaru Menteng Orangutan Reintroduction Center and Camp Bulu, both funded by the Orangutan Foundation.

VANISHING FORESTS

The biggest threat to orangutans is the loss of their habitat — the place where they live. The rainforests of Southeast Asia are the oldest rainforests on Earth but, because of human activity, they are rapidly disappearing.

The forest trees have been cut down for their wood, which can be used to make furniture or paper, and to make space for new settlements. The biggest cause of deforestation – the destruction of forests – is clearing land for oil palm plantations. Oil palm fruit is crushed to make palm oil.

Fact File: Palm Oil

There is a huge demand for palm oil around the world. It is an ingredient in many different processed foods, from chocolate and chips to margarine and cream cheese. It is also used to manufacture makeup and for biodiesel (an alternative fuel for cars).

Deforestation is so terrible that in Indonesia less than half of the original rainforest remains. It is a similar story in Malaysia. Orangutan rescue groups and other environmental campaigners are fighting to save the rainforests. The forests are home to around 3,000 species, including rare tigers and rhinos.

7

THE PET TRADE

Another problem that faces orangutans is the pet trade. Orangutan babies are very appealing because their faces look so human. That makes people wrongly believe that they will make adorable pets.

Trade in orangutans is illegal but sadly this does not stop people from hunting them. A few are killed for their meat, but most are caught for the pet trade. Babies are taken away from their mothers, who are usually killed, and then sold. Some are bought by wealthy locals. Others are flown or shipped to international buyers. The buyers think they will make unusual and impressive pets.

Most orangutan pets receive good care – somewhere clean to live, regular meals, and plenty of attention and affection. Unfortunately, once the orangutans reach the age of about five, they stop being cute and gentle. Their behavior becomes hard to predict or even aggressive. By now, the pet orangutans are also much stronger than their owners. Many are abandoned at this stage. Orangutan rehabilitation centers work to find new homes for these animals.

Some orangutan orphans are rescued at the age of just a few months. Others arrive at centers when they are a few years old. Whatever their age, they are lost without their mothers. Orangutans are among the animals that take longest to grow up.

One reason why orangutan babies rely on their mothers so much is because of the orangutan way of life. Unlike most primates, orangutans do not live in groups or communities. They are loners. So a baby has only its mother to teach it all the survival skills it needs.

For the first six months of life, an orangutan clings to its mother and depends on her for food and warmth. Later, the mother teaches her offspring where to find the best food or how to build a nighttime nest. The orangutan stays with its mom for eight or nine years.

Fact File: Having Babies

Orangutan dads are not involved in rearing youngsters. The parents mate, then go their separate ways. After an eight-month pregnancy, the mother gives birth to one baby or, very occasionally, twins. During her lifetime, a female orangutan raises between three and five young.

Mother Peta carries her baby daughter, Petra, at Camp Leakey.

CARETAKERS

People do many different, important jobs at the rescue and rehabilitation centers. There is usually at least one vet, who can give them medical care. There may be researchers, finding out more about orangutans. And at the heart of each center are the caretakers.

The caretakers are usually a mix of paid staff and volunteers. The paid staff are people who live locally or on site. The volunteers are often students or other young people who are traveling and stop off at the center for a few weeks to help. They are not paid, but they do receive a place to stay and the amazing opportunity to get to know orangutans up close.

The caretakers at the rescue centers have to take on the roles of orangutan mothers. They feed the orphans, and keep them warm and safe. They give them somewhere comfortable to sleep. They also give the animals emotional support. Orangutans are closely related to humans and show signs of having similar feelings. They form strong bonds and relationships, both with each other and with the caretakers.

DINNERTIME

Orangutans are mammals. For the first three months of their lives, the only thing that wild orangutan babies eat or drink is their mothers' milk. Then they start to move on to solid foods. As adults, orangutans mostly eat fruit.

Caretakers at the rehabilitation centers bottle-feed the babies with formula milk. When the infants are around three months old, the carers start to give them soft fruit. Orangutan mothers pre-chew their babies' food. The carers copy this by mashing the fruit. It looks similar to human baby food.

Fact File: Plant Foods

Orangutans feed on the leaves, stems, and fruits of more than 400 different plants. In the wild, they would learn which foods are safe by watching their mothers. Orphans learn this from the carers or older orphans. A favorite food is the durian fruit. The orangutans use leaves like gloves when they handle this spiny fruit.

Slowly, the caretakers introduce a variety of foods. Between the ages of three and seven, juvenile orangutans move on to solid food. They eat on feeding platforms, and gradually give up their milk feeds. In the wild, they will have to spend up to six hours a day eating or foraging.

PLAYTIME

Like all animal babies, young orangutans learn a lot through play. Games allow them to practice many skills that will be useful in adult life. The orangutans copy the actions of the other orangutans or caretakers — just like human children playing make-believe.

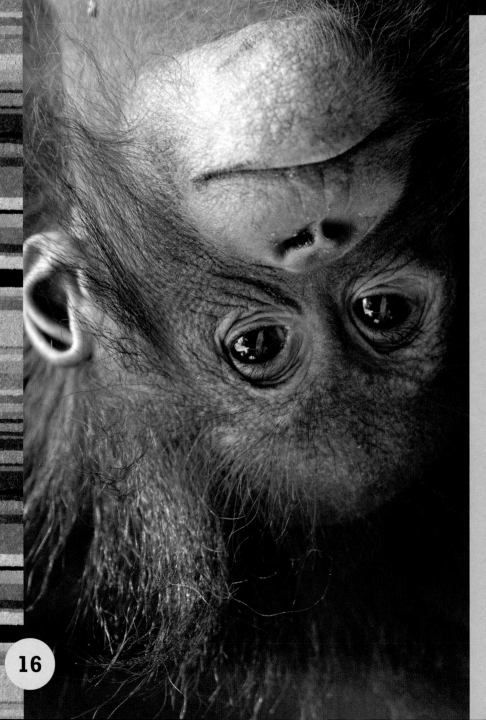

Adult orangutans are quite slow and clumsy on the ground. When they're up in the trees, however, their acrobatics are amazing. No wonder orangutans so rarely come down to the forest floor. Orangutans learn their swinging technique as youngsters playing "chase." Caretakers at rescue centers make sure that young orangutans can learn and practice these same skills, so that they can one day return to the wild.

As infants, orangutans also try out more precise movements and skills. A branch is a very useful toy. Youngsters learn to pluck off the leaves, which can be eaten or used to line a nest, until they are left with a thin, bendy stick. Sticks are useful tools for many jobs – for example, adults use them to "fish" honey from honeycomb. Orangutans are very clever!

A male Bornean orangutan baby, Thor, plays with a leaf stem at Camp Leakey.

Orangutans need more sleep than humans. Like us, however, they are active when it is light and rest when it is dark. The adults sleep for around 14 hours a night. Babies need more sleep than adults.

In the wild, infants share their mothers' nests. At the rescue and rehabilitation centers, the young orangutans sometimes nap cuddled up to a caretaker. The caretakers do not snuggle up with the orphans at night, though. Instead, they give the orangutans teddy bears or soft blankets that they can hold as they sleep in their hammocks.

A juvenile relaxes at Nyaru Menteng Orangutan Reintroduction Project.

Like their ape relatives gorillas and chimpanzees, wild orangutans sleep in treetop nests. Amazingly, they build themselves a new one every evening. Each day, the orangutans move through the forest in search of food. When night falls, they camp wherever they find themselves, rather than returning to the same spot.

Fact File: Night Nests

Orangutans make their nests at sunset. It can take half an hour. First, they select a suitable branch. This is usually 60 to 90 feet (18 to 28 m) high. Next, they weave together small branches. Finally, they add some soft leaves.

KEEPING CLEAN

In the wild, orangutans learn how to groom themselves from their mother as she picks through their fur. At the center, the carers show them how to bathe and groom. They also copy what the older orangutans are doing.

Grooming is a long, slow process. The orangutans use their fingernails and toenails to carefully "comb" through their own hair. They clean it with their lips and tongues. Grooming stops the hair from getting tangled, but its main purpose is to get rid of annoying, itchy parasites. Whenever the orangutan finds one, it pops it into its mouth and eats it – delicious!

Bathtime at the Orangutan Care Center

In the wild, orangutans do not take baths very often. They sometimes cool off in a shallow pool or river, but they stay near the bank. They do not want to become lunch for a hungry crocodile! Very occasionally, orangutans break this rule and wade right across a river or pool – but only if there's some really tempting food on the other side.

21

BEING FRIENDLY

In the wild, orangutans do not appear to live in large groups like other apes. Every male has his own territory, which no other males are allowed into. Females have their own home ranges too.

Females are more sociable than males. They live with their young for many years. When daughters leave home, they often set up their own home ranges near their mothers. Females sometimes eat together too. It seems they do have a kind of community – one where they live apart and have plenty of time alone!

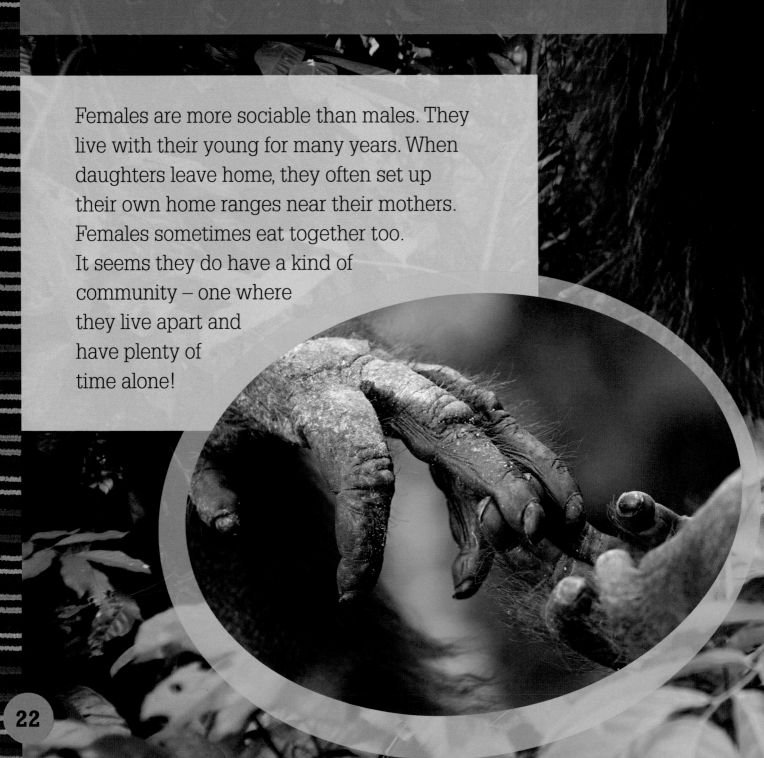

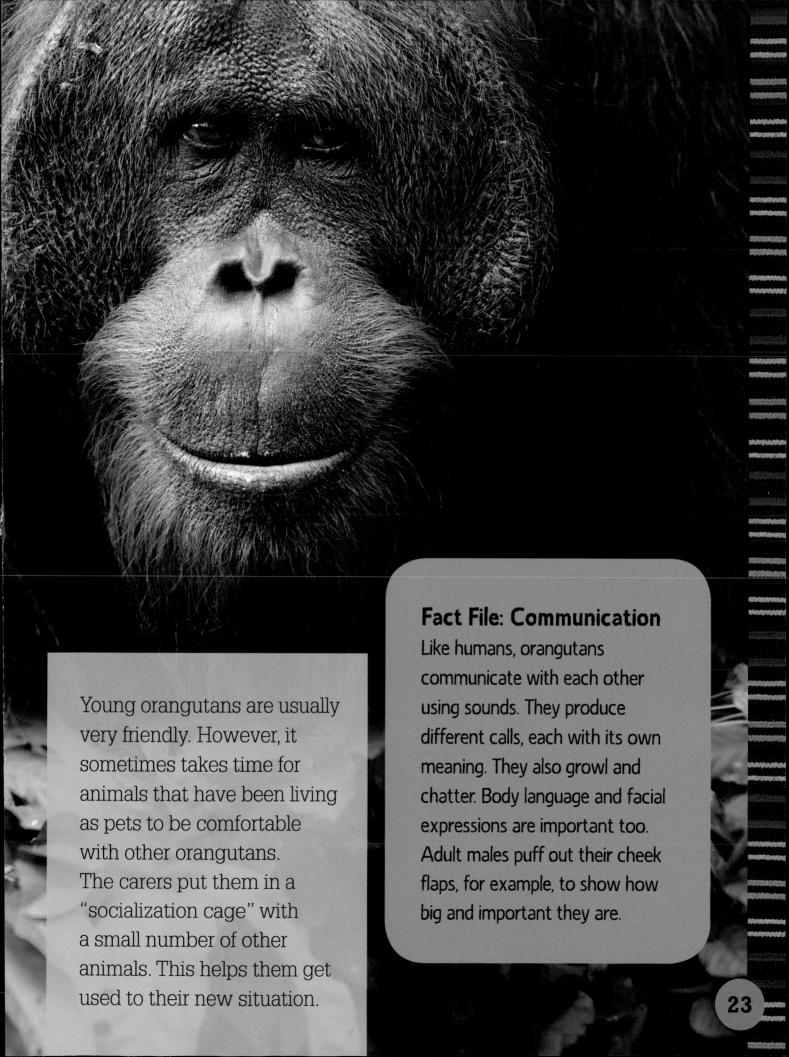

Young orangutans are usually very friendly. However, it sometimes takes time for animals that have been living as pets to be comfortable with other orangutans. The carers put them in a "socialization cage" with a small number of other animals. This helps them get used to their new situation.

Fact File: Communication

Like humans, orangutans communicate with each other using sounds. They produce different calls, each with its own meaning. They also growl and chatter. Body language and facial expressions are important too. Adult males puff out their cheek flaps, for example, to show how big and important they are.

FOREST SKILLS

The name orangutan means "person of the forest." Before the caretakers will release apes back into the wild, they need to be sure that they have the skills to survive out in the forest.

Some skills are built in. For example, the way that orangutans swing through the trees, hand over hand, seems to be something that they know how to do from birth. As they grow up, the more they practice, the better at swinging they get. Orangutans also learn a lot by copying. In the wild, the mother is the role model. At the center, youngsters watch what the other orangutans do.

No one expects the young orangutans to go straight into the forest from the safety of the center and fend for themselves. Caretakers spend time preparing them. They take them on walks in the forest so that they can get used to the sights, smells and sounds. The orangutans learn to "read" their surroundings and recognize which animal calls are a clue that danger is nearby.

Exploring the forest together: a caretaker and juvenile at the Orangutan Care Center

BACK TO THE WILD

When orangutans first arrive at the center, they are put into quarantine — a place separate from the other animals. Next, they spend time in the socialization cages and later, there are trips into the forest. The final stage before release is the "halfway" cage.

Most centers keep large cages out in the forest where orangutans can live safe from predators. In these enormous "halfway" cages, the animals get used to the idea of being back in the wild. They swing among the trees and forage for food. The caretakers bring extra food too.

The caretakers want their rehabilitated apes to have the best chance of survival. It is a challenge to find suitable places to release them. The center at Nyaru Menteng has bought its own 900,000-acre (400,000 hectare) area of rainforest, into which it has released more than 80 orangutans so far.

Fact File: Microchipping

All the rehabilitation centers microchip their orangutans. This means that they implant a tiny silicon chip under the ape's skin. The chip holds a number that is unique to that orangutan and that can be matched back to its medical records.

SPREADING THE WORD

The rehabilitation center's main job is rescuing orangutans and preparing them to be released back into the wild. The hope is that these animals will go on to have babies of their own.

The centers also work hard to educate people about orangutans and the dangers they face, so that they value them more. The centers try to show people how important it is to all of us that we save the rainforests of Southeast Asia. In particular, they educate local people, so that they will not be tempted to hunt orangutans for meat or sell them as pets.

It can be hard to persuade local people, who may be very poor, that it is a bad idea to make money by hunting orangutans. The centers are showing how tourism could be the answer. Tourists pay a lot of money to see orangutans. This money helps to fund conservation work (protecting their habitat). At the same time, looking after the tourists brings jobs for local people.

GLOSSARY

ANTHROPOLOGIST A scientist who studies the story of human life on Earth.

CONSERVATION Protecting and keeping for the future.

DEFORESTATION Chopping down an area's forests.

FORAGE To search for food.

GREAT APE An animal belonging to the hominid family, which includes gorillas, chimpanzees and orangutans.

HABITAT The place where an animal or plant lives.

HOME RANGE The area over which an animal travels in its searches for food and a mate.

ILLEGAL Against the law.

MAMMALS Animals with warm blood that give birth to live young, which they feed with milk.

NATIONAL PARK An area where the land is protected by law so that it stays wild.

ORPHANED Having lost its parents.

PARASITE An animal or plant that survives by living off another animal or plant.

PLANTATION A huge farm where one crop is grown for sale.

PREDATOR An animal that survives by hunting, killing, and eating other animals.

PRIMATE Belonging to the group of animals that includes humans, apes and monkeys.

PROCESSED FOOD Food that has been produced in a factory.

RAINFOREST A thick tropical forest where there is heavy rainfall.

REHABILITATION Being prepared to live a normal life.

RESERVE An area where the land and its wildlife are being saved for the future, by the government or an organization.

SOCIALIZATION Making an animal used to being with others of its kind.

TERRITORY The area over which an animal travels in its searches for food and a mate, and which that animal defends against others.

VOLUNTEER Someone who works for free. Volunteers at rehabilitation centers usually receive free lodging.

FURTHER INFORMATION

FURTHER READING

100 Facts: Monkeys and Apes by Camilla de la Bedoyere
    (Miles Kelly Publishing, 2010)

A Day in the Life: Rainforest Animals: Orangutan by Anita Ganeri
    (Raintree, 2011)

DK Readers: Ape Adventures by Catherine Chambers
    (Dorling Kindersley, 2013)

Exploring Nature: Great Apes by Barbara Taylor (Armadillo Music, 2014)

Face to Face with Orangutans by Tim Laman and Cheryl Knott
    (National Geographic Society, 2009)

Orangutan by Suzi Eszterhas (Frances Lincoln Children's Books, 2013)

WEBSITES

Due to the changing nature of Internet links, PowerKids Press has developed
an online list of websites related to the subject of this book. This site is updated
regularly. Please use this link to access the list:
www.powerkidslinks.com/sta/orang

INDEX